PAPERBACK SONGS

CHRISTMAS SONGS

**MELODY LINE, CHORDS AND LYRICS
FOR KEYBOARD • GUITAR • VOCAL**

HAL•LEONARD®

ISBN 0-634-04741-8

HAL•LEONARD®
CORPORATION
7777 W. BLUEMOUND RD. P.O. BOX 13819 MILWAUKEE, WI 53213

Visit Hal Leonard Online at
www.halleonard.com

Printed in Canada

Welcome to the PAPERBACK SONGS SERIES.

Do you play piano, guitar, electronic keyboard, sing or play any instrument for that matter? If so, this handy "pocket tune" book is for you.

The concise, one-line music notation consists of:

MELODY, LYRICS & CHORD SYMBOLS

Whether strumming the chords on guitar, "faking" an arrangement on piano/keyboard or singing the lyrics, these fake book style arrangements can be enjoyed at any experience level – hobbyist to professional.

The musical skills necessary to successfully use this book are minimal. If you play guitar and need some help with chords, a basic chord chart is included at the back of the book.

While playing and singing is the first thing that comes to mind when using this book, it can also serve as a compact, comprehensive reference guide.

However you choose to use this PAPERBACK SONGS SERIES book, by all means have fun!

CONTENTS

ALL I WANT FOR CHRISTMAS IS YOU

Words and Music by MARIAH CAREY
and WALTER AFANASIEFF

8

1. baby. ___ Oh, ___ *2.* baby. ___ Oh, ___

All the lights ___ are shin - ing so

bright - ly ev - 'ry - where, ___

and the sound ___ of chil - dren's

laugh - ter fills ___ the air, ___

And ev - 'ry - one ___ is sing - ing,

I hear those sleigh ___ bells ring - ing.

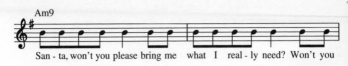

San - ta, won't you please bring me what I real - ly need? Won't you

D.S. al Coda

please bring my ba - by to me?_____ Oh, __

CODA

all I want for Christ - mas _____

is _____ you. _____

(Ooh, _____ ba - by.) __

All I want for Christ - mas is

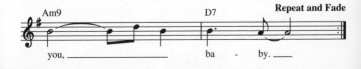

Repeat and Fade

you, _____ ba - by. __

AS LONG AS
THERE'S CHRISTMAS

from Walt Disney's
BEAUTY AND THE BEAST - THE ENCHANTED CHRISTMAS

Music by RACHEL PORTMAN
Lyrics by DON BLACK

Flowing

Female: There is more _____ to this

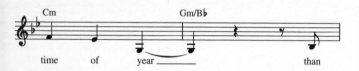

time of year _____ than

sleigh - bells and hol - ly,

Male: mis - tle - toe and snow.

Freely

Both: Those things will come and go.

Tempo I

Female: Don't look in - side _____ a stock - ing. Don't look un - der _____ the tree. The one thing we're _____ look - ing for is some - thing we can't see. _____ *Male:* Far more pre - cious _____ than sil - ver and more splen - did _____ than gold, _____ this is some - thing to

geth - er, it's a time ___ to ___ re -

joice. ___ *Female:* And though we ___ may look

dif - f'rent, *Both:* we'll all sing with ___ one

voice. *Male:* Whoa. ___

___ *Both:* As long as there's

Christ - mas, I tru - ly be -

lieve that hope is the

14

C-H-R-I-S-T-M-A-S

Words by JENNY LOU CARSON
Music by EDDY ARNOLD

Moderately

When I was but a young-ster

Christ-mas meant one thing, That

I'd be get-ting lots of toys that

day. _____ I

learned a whole lot dif-f'rent when

moth-er sat me down And

taught me to spell Christ-mas this

18

BABY, IT'S COLD OUTSIDE

from the Motion Picture NEPTUNE'S DAUGHTER

By FRANK LOESSER

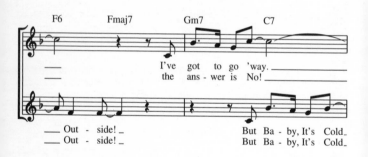

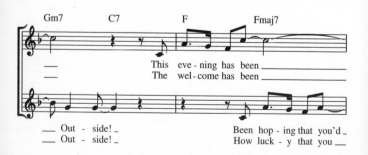

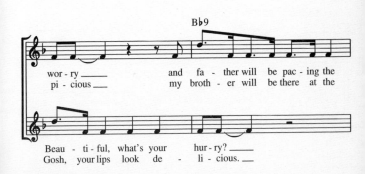

F6

floor.   So   real - ly I'd   bet - ter
door.   My maid - en aunt's mind   is

Lis - ten to the fi - re-place roar!
waves up-on a trop - ic - al shore!

G7

scur - ry, _____   well, may - be just a half a drink
vi - cious _____   well, may - be just a cig - a - rette

Beau - ti - ful, please, don't hur - ry. _____
Gosh, your lips are de - li - cious _____

C7

more.   The
more.   I've

Put   some re - cords on   while I   pour. _____
nev - er such   a bliz - zard be - fore. _____

F   **Fmaj7**

neigh - bors might think _____
got   to   get   home _____

_____   But, ba - by, it's bad _____
_____   But, ba - by, you'd freeze _____

Bb6

I ought to say "No, no,
There's bound to be talk to -

your hair looks swell. _____
this thing to me. _____

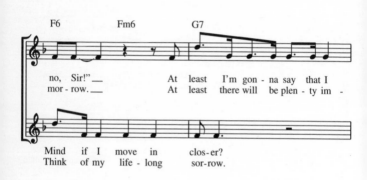

F6   Fm6   G7

no, Sir!" ___   At least I'm gon - na say that I
mor - row. ___   At least there will be plen - ty im -

Mind if I move in clos-er?
Think of my life - long sor-row.

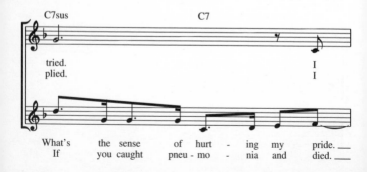

C7sus   C7

tried.   I
plied.   I

What's the sense of hurt - ing my pride. ___
If you caught pneu - mo - nia and died. ___

BECAUSE IT'S CHRISTMAS
(For All the Children)

Music by BARRY MANILOW
Lyric by BRUCE SUSSMAN and JACK FELDMAN

Moderately slow

To-night the stars _ shine _ for the chil - dren
To-night be-longs _ to _ all the chil - dren,

and light the way for dreams to fly.
to - night their joy rings through the air.

To-night our love comes wrapped in _ rib - bons,
And so, we send our ten - der bless - ings

the world is right and hopes are high.
to all the chil - dren ev - 'ry - where

And from a dark _ and frost - ed
to see the smiles _ and hear the

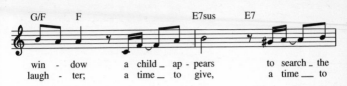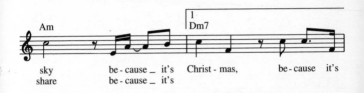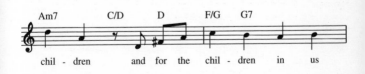

27

win - dow a child _ ap - pears to search _ the
laugh - ter; a time _ to give, a time __ to

sky be - cause _ it's Christ - mas, be - cause it's
share be - cause _ it's

Christ - mas. Christ - mas for now _ and for -

ev - er, for all ___ of the

chil - dren and for the chil - dren in us

all. *(Instrumental)*

To-night be-longs_ to all the chil - dren,

to - night _ their joy rings_ through the air.

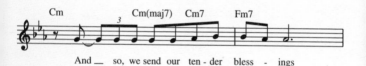

And _ so, we send our ten - der bless - ings

to all ___ the chil - dren ___ ev - 'ry-

where to see the smiles_ and hear the

laugh - ter; a time_ to give, a time_ to

29

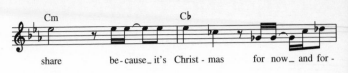

share be - cause _ it's Christ - mas for now _ and for -

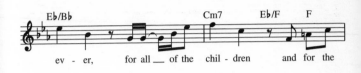

ev - er, for all __ of the chil - dren and for the

chil - dren in us

all. _____ *(Instrumental)*
(Vocal 1st time only)

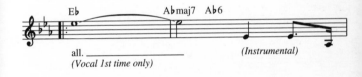

Repeat and Fade

CAROLING, CAROLING

Words by WIHLA HUTSON
Music by ALFRED BURT

With a lilt

Car - ol - ing, Car - ol - ing, now we go;
Car - ol - ing, Car - ol - ing, thru the town;

Christ - mas bells are ring - ing! Car - ol - ing, Car - ol - ing,
Christ - mas bells are ring - ing! Car - ol - ing, Car - ol - ing,

thru the snow; Christ - mas bells are ring - ing!
up and down; Christ - mas bells are ring - ing!

Joy - ous voic - es sweet and clear,
Mark ye well the song we sing,

Sing and sad of heart to cheer. Ding, dong,
Glad - some tid - ings now we bring. Ding, dong,

ding, dong, Christ - mas bells are ring - ing!
ding, dong, Christ - mas bells are ring - ing!

THE CHIPMUNK SONG

Words and Music by
ROSS BAGDASARIAN

THE CHRISTMAS SHOES

Words and Music by LEONARD AHLSTROM
and EDDIE CARSWELL

Moderately

It was al - most Christ - mas time; __

there I stood in an - oth - er line, __

tryin' to buy that last gift or two, __

not real - ly in the Christ - mas mood. __

Stand - in' right in front __ of me was a

lit - tle boy wait - ing anx - ious - ly,

pac - in' 'round like lit - tle boys do, ___

and in his hands he held ___ a pair of

shoes. And his

clothes were worn and old, ___ he was

dirt - y from head to toe. ___ But

when it came _ his time ___ to pay, _ I

could - n't be - lieve ___ what I heard him say.

"Sir, I wan-na buy these shoes

for my ma-ma, please.

It's Christ-mas Eve _ and these

shoes are just her _ size.

Could you hur - ry, sir? _

Dad - dy says there's not much time. _

You see, she's been sick for quite_

_ a while _ and I know these shoes will make_

___ her smile ___ and I want her to look beau-

-ti-ful ___ if Ma - ma ___ meets

Je - sus ___ to - night."

They count-ed

pen-nies for ___ what seemed ___ like years, ___ then the

cash-ier said, "Son, there's not e-nough here." ___

He searched his pock-ets fran - ti-c'lly, _

then he turned and he looked at me. ___ He said,

THE CHRISTMAS SONG

(Chestnuts Roasting on an Open Fire)

Music and Lyric by MEL TORME
and ROBERT WELLS

Chest - nuts roast - ing on an o - pen fire,

Jack Frost nip - ping at your nose.

Yule - tide car - ols be - ing sung by a choir and

folks dressed up like Es - ki - mos. Ev - 'ry - bod - y

knows a tur - key and some mis - tle - toe _____

help to make the sea - son bright. Ti - ny tots with their

eyes all a - glow will find it hard to sleep to -

41

CHRISTMAS TIME IS HERE

from *A CHARLIE BROWN CHRISTMAS*

Words by LEE MENDELSON
Music by VINCE GUARALDI

Slowly

Christ-mas time is here, hap-pi-ness and

cheer, fun for all, that chil-dren call their

fa - v'rite time of year. Snow-flakes in the

air, car-ols ev - 'ry - where,

old - en times and an-cient rhymes of love, and dreams to

share. Sleigh bells in the air, beau-ty ev - 'ry -

where, Yule-tide by the fire - side, and

joy - ful mem - 'ries there. Christ-mas time is here,

fam - 'lies draw - ing near, oh, that we could

al - ways see such spir - it through the year.

44

THE CHRISTMAS WALTZ

Words by SAMMY CAHN
Music by JULE STYNE

Moderately, with expression

Frost - ed win - dow panes, ___ can - dles

gleam - ing in - side, Paint - ed can - dy canes ___

___ on the tree; San - ta's

on his way, he's filled his sleigh with

things, ___ Things for you and for

me. It's that time of year, ___ When the

COLD DECEMBER NIGHTS

Words and Music by MICHAEL McCARY
and SHAWN STOCKMAN

Moderately slow

Cold De-cem-ber nights like this makes me
The stars shine bright as the night air, and the

real-ly scared.
thought of you not be-ing here

You're not
makes me

real-ly there
shed a tear.

and my
And yet

tree is real-ly bare. An-oth-er lone-
mat-ters re-main un-clear 'bout why you're gone,

-ly night, no gifts, no toys un-der-
or if you'll ev-er re-turn to this

neath my tree.
bro-ken heart.

Can this
Life is

Am9   Gsus2/B   C

real - ly __ be? _____ I'm sing-ing
so torn __ a - part _____ and God

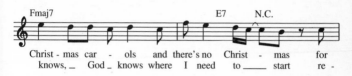

Fmaj7   E7   N.C.

Christ - mas car - ols and there's no Christ - mas for
knows, __ God __ knows where I need to __ start re -

Am9   Gsus2/B

me? _____
build - ing. _____

C   Fmaj7

Why aren't __ you next __ to me _____

Am9   Gsus2/B

cel - e - brat - ing Christ - mas? ____

C   Fmaj7

Why can't __ you see _____ what hurts so bad? __

Am9   Gsus2/B

_____ Whoa. _____

48

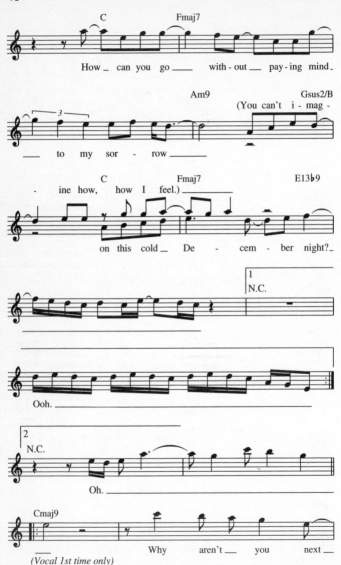

49

DO THEY KNOW IT'S CHRISTMAS?

Words and Music by M. URE
and B. GELDOF

bit - ter sting of tears. And the
Christ - mas bells _ that ring _ there _ are the
clang - ing chimes of doom. _ Well, to -
night thank God it's them _ in - stead of
you. And there
won't be snow _ in Af - ri - ca _ this Christ -
- mas - time; _ the
great - est gift _ they'll get this year _ is life. _

54

EMMANUEL

Words and Music by
MICHAEL W. SMITH

Em - man - u - el, Em -

man - u - el.

Won - der - ful Coun - sel - or, _____

Lord of life, Lord of all. _____ He's _ the

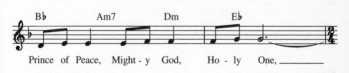

Prince of Peace, Might - y God, Ho - ly One, _____

To Coda ⊕

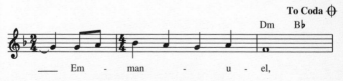

___ Em - man - u - el,

DO YOU HEAR WHAT I HEAR

Words and Music by NOEL REGNEY
and GLORIA SHAYNE

Moderately, with feeling

Said the night wind to the lit-tle lamb,
lit-tle lamb to the shep-herd boy,
shep-herd boy to the might-y king,
king to the peo-ple ev-'ry-where,

"Do you see what I see? _____
"Do you hear what I hear? _____
"Do you know what I know? _____
"Lis-ten to what I say! _____

Way up in the sky, lit-tle lamb,
Ring-ing through the sky, shep-herd boy,
In your pal-ace warm, might-y king,
Pray for peace, _ peo-ple ev-'ry-where,

do you see what I see? _____
do you hear what I hear? _____
do you know what I know? _____
lis-ten to what I say! _____

star, a star, danc-ing in the night, with a
song, a song, high a-bove the tree, with a
Child, a Child shiv-ers in the cold; let us
Child, the Child, sleep-ing in the night, He will

FELIZ NAVIDAD

Music and Lyrics by
JOSE FELICIANO

Moderately

Fe - liz Na - vi - dad. _____

Fe - liz Na - vi - dad. _____

Fe - liz Na - vi - dad. Pros - pe - ro

a - ño y fe - li - ci - dad. _____

Fe - liz Na - vi - ___

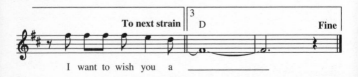

To next strain

I want to wish you a _____

61

Mer - ry Christ-mas, with lots of pres - ents to make you hap - py. I want to wish you a Mer - ry Christ-mas from the bot - tom of my heart. _____ I want to wish you a Mer - ry Christ-mas, with mis - tle - toe and __ lots of cheer. _ With lots of laugh-ter through-out the years from the bot - tom of my heart. _____ Fe - liz Na - vi -

D.S. al Fine

FROSTY THE SNOW MAN

Words and Music by STEVE NELSON
and JACK ROLLINS

| F | | | | C | Am | A7 |

made of snow but the chil-dren know __ how he
here and there all a - round the square, _ say - in',

| Dm7 | G7 | C |

came to life one day. There
"Catch me if you can." He

| F | | C |

must have been some mag - ic in that
led them down the streets of town right

| Dm7 | G7 | C |

old silk hat they found, For
to the traf - fic cop, And he

| G | | Ddim |

when they placed it on his head he be -
on - ly paused a mo - ment when __ he

| Am7 | D7 | G | G7 |

gan to dance a - round. Oh,
heard him hol - ler, "Stop!" For

| C | | C7 |

Frost - y The Snow Man was a -
Frost - y The Snow Man had to

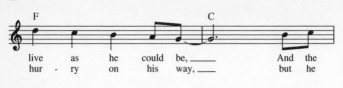

F · · · · · C
live   as   he   could be, _____   And the
hur - ry   on   his   way, _____   but he

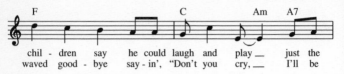

F · · · · · C · Am · A7
chil - dren say   he could laugh and play __ just the
waved good - bye say - in', "Don't you cry, __   I'll be

Dm7 · G7 · C
same   as   you   and   me.
back   a - gain some - day."

C
Thump - et - y   thump thump,   thump - et - y   thump thump.

G7
Look   at   Frost - y   go.

Thump - et - y   thump thump,   thump - et - y   thump thump.

C
O - ver   the   hills   of   snow.

GRANDMA GOT RUN OVER BY A REINDEER

Words and Music by
RANDY BROOKS

Moderately bright

Chorus

Grand-ma Got Run O - ver By A Rein-deer

walk - ing home from our house Christ-mas Eve.

You can say there's no such thing as San - ta, but

To Coda

as for me and Grand-pa, we be - lieve.

Verse

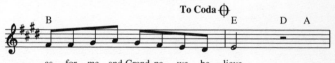

1. She'd been drink-ing too much egg - nog
2., 3. *(See additional lyrics)*

and we begged her not to go,

66

but she for-got her med - i - ca-tion, and she

stag-gered out the door in - to the snow.

When we found her Christ-mas morn-ing

at the scene of the at - tack,

she had hoof-prints on her fore-head, and in -

1st and 2nd time D.C.
3rd time D.C. al Coda

crim - i - nat - ing Claus marks on her back.

CODA

lieve. Grand-ma Got Run O - ver By A

Rein-deer   walk-ing home from our house Christ-mas

B

Eve.   You can say there's no such thing as

F#   C#

San-ta,   but as for me and Grand-pa, we be-

F#   C#   F#

lieve. _____

Additional Lyrics

2. Now we're all so proud of Grandpa,
   He's been taking this so well.
   See him in there watching football,
   Drinking beer and playing cards with Cousin Mel.
   It's not Christmas without Grandma.
   All the family's dressed in black,
   And we just can't help but wonder:
   Should we open up her gifts or send them back?
   Chorus

3. Now the goose is on the table,
   And the pudding made of fig,
   And the blue and silver candles,
   That would just have matched the hair in Grandma's wig.
   I've warned all my friends and neighbors,
   Better watch out for yourselves.
   They should never give a license
   To a man who drives a sleigh and plays with elves.
   Chorus

THE GIFT

Words and Music by TOM DOUGLAS
and JIM BRICKMAN

Slow Ballad

Female: Win-ter snow is fall-ing __ down,

chil-dren laugh-ing all a-round,

lights are turn-ing on, _____ like a

fair-y tale __ come true. __

Sit-ting by the fire __ we made,

you're the an-swer when I prayed __

ev - 'ry day ___ for the

gift. *(Instrumental)*

Male: Watch - ing as you

soft - ly ___ sleep, what I'd give if

I could ___ keep just this mo -

- ment, if on - ly time ___ stood

still. But the col - ors fade ___

72

73

GRANDMA'S
KILLER FRUITCAKE

Words and Music by ELMO SHROPSHIRE
and RITA ABRAMS

Country Polka

G

1. The hol-i-days were up-on us and
2., 3. *(See additional lyrics)*

C   G

things were go-in' fine, 'til the day I heard the

A7   D7

door-bell and a chill ran up my spine. I

G   C

grabbed the wife and chil-dren as the post-man wheeled it

G

in. A year-ly Christ-mas night-mare has

Chorus

A7   D7   G

just came back a-gain. It was hard-er than the head of

C

Un-cle Buck-y, heav-y as a Ser-mon of

G

Preach - er Luck - y.   One's e - nough to give the whole

A7

state   of Ken - tuck - y   a   great   big   bel - ly -

D7   G

ache.   It was dens-er than a drove of   barn-yard tur-keys,

C   G

tough - er than a truck - load of   all - beef   jerk - y.

A   D

Dri-er than a drought in   Al - bu-quer-que, Grand-ma's Kill-er Fruit -

1, 2
G

3
G

cake.   2. Now   cake.
3. It's

Additional Lyrics

2. Now I've had to swallow some marginal fare at our family feast.
   I even downed Aunt Dolly's possom pie just to keep the family peace.
   I winced at Wilma's gizzard mousse, but said it tasted fine,
   But that lethal weapon that Grandma bakes is where I draw the line.
   Chorus

3. It's early Christmas morning, the phone rings us awake.
   It's Grandma, Pa, she wants to know how'd we liked the cake.
   "Well, Grandma, I never. Uh, we couldn't.
   It was, uh, unbelievable, that's for shore.
   What's that you say? Oh, no Grandma, Puh-leeez don't send us more!"
   Chorus

THE GREATEST GIFT OF ALL

Words and Music by
JOHN JARVIS

Moderately slow

G   D/F♯   G

Dawn is slow - ly break - ing, __

C   G

our friends have all _____ gone home.

D/F♯   Em

You and I are wait - ing __

A7   D

for San - ta Claus to come.

G   D/F♯   G   G7

There's a pres - ent by _____ the tree,

C   G

stock - ings on the wall.

Know-ing you're in love with me is The

Great - est Gift Of _ All.

The fire is slow - ly fad - ing, ____

chill is in the air.

All the gifts are wait - ing ____

for chil - dren ev - 'ry - where.

Through the win - dow I ____ can see __

GREENWILLOW CHRISTMAS

from GREENWILLOW

By FRANK LOESSER

GROWN-UP
CHRISTMAS LIST

Words and Music by DAVID FOSTER
and LINDA THOMPSON-JENNER

Bm7   Em7   G/D   Csus2   D7sus

____ and time would heal _ all hearts.

G   Bm7/E   Em/D   C(add9) C   Am7   Am7/D

And ev-'ry-one would have _ a friend, _ and right would al-ways

Bm7   Em7   G/D   C#m7b5 F#7b9 F#7#5

win,   and love would nev - er   end. _____

Bm7   Em   Am7   Am7/D |1 G C/G D/G G   B7/D#

This is my grown-up Christ - mas list.   *(Instrumental)*

Em   G/B   C   Am7   Dsus   D   D/C

As

|2 G   C/G D/G G   G7sus

list. ____   What is _ this il - lu - sion called?

Dm/C   C Dm/C C   Em7   Em7/A   A

The in-no-cence of youth. _   May-be on - ly in _ our blind be-lief _

D   F#sus F#   B   F#   G#m

can we ev-er find _ the truth.   *(Instrumental)*

84

HAPPY CHRISTMAS, LITTLE FRIEND

Lyrics by OSCAR HAMMERSTEIN II
Music by RICHARD RODGERS

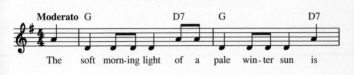

The soft morn-ing light of a pale win-ter sun is

trac - ing the trees on the snow, Leap

up lit - tle friend and fly down the stairs For

Christ - mas is wait - ing be - low. There's a

tree in the room run - ning o - ver with stars that

twin - kle and sing to your eyes And

under the tree there are pres-ents that say Un-

wrap me and get a sur - prise. ____

____ Hap - py

Christ - mas, Lit - tle Friend, May your heart be

laugh - ing all day. ____ May your

joy be a dream you'll re - mem - ber, ____ As the

years roll a - long on their way. ____ As the

years roll a - long on their way _____ You'll be

show - ing your own kid a tree. _____

Then at last, my friend, you'll know How_

hap - py a Christ - mas can be, _____ How

hap - py a Christ - mas can

1

be. _____

2

be. _____

HAPPY HOLIDAY

from the Motion Picture Irving Berlin's HOLIDAY INN

Words and Music by
IRVING BERLIN

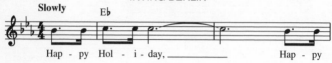

Hap - py Hol - i - day, _____ Hap - py

Hol - i - day. _____ While the

mer - ry bells keep ring - ing, may your

ev - 'ry wish come true. Hap - py

Hol - i - day, _____ Hap - py Hol - i - day. _____

_____ May the cal - en - dar keep

bring - ing hap - py hol - i - days to

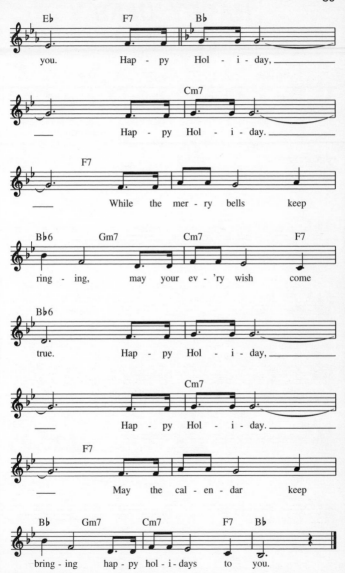

HAPPY XMAS
(War Is Over)

Words and Music by JOHN LENNON
and YOKO ONO

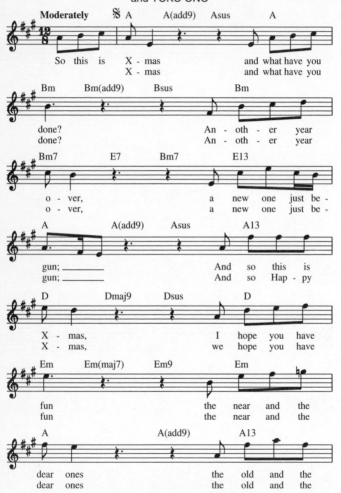

91

Em Em(maj7) Em9 Em
white for the yel - low and
if you want it
A7sus A7 Em7 A7
red ones let's stop all the
war is o - ver
D A7 Em D13
fights. A mer - ry, mer - ry
now.)
G
X - mas and a hap - py New
A G F♯m Em G
Year, let's hope it's a good one with-out an - y
D.S. al Coda
CODA
D E E13
fear. And so this is
D E
fear.
A Amaj7 D6 A Bm Bm(maj7) Bm9 Bm
War is o - ver if you want it
E7sus E7 Bm7 E7 A E7 Bm A
war is o - ver now.

HOLLY LEAVES
AND CHRISTMAS TREES

Words and Music by RED WEST
and GLEN SPREEN

94

Am | Dm

Christ-mas seems _____ to come and go, ___

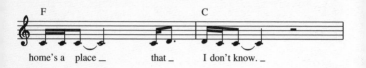

F | C

home's a place _ that _ I don't know. _

G | C

Hol-ly Leaves _____ And Christ-mas Trees, _

G | C

it's that time _ of year, _____

Am | Em

lights a-glow _ and mis-tle-toe _____ don't

F | G

mean a thing _____ when you're not here.

As I walk, _ walk this lone-ly street, _____ the

sound of snow _ be - neath my feet, _____ I

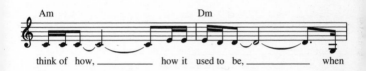

think of how, _____ how it used to be, _____ when

Hol-ly Leaves _ And Christ-mas Trees _

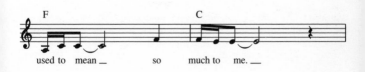

used to mean _ so much to me. _

A HOLLY
JOLLY CHRISTMAS

Music and Lyrics by
JOHNNY MARKS

Moderately bright

Have a Hol – ly Jol – ly Christ - mas, it's the
Hol – ly Jol – ly Christ - mas, and when

best time of the year. _____
you walk down the street _____

I don't know if there'll be snow but
Say hel – lo to friends you know and

have a cup of cheer. __ Have a

ev – 'ry – one you meet.

Oh, ho, the mis – tle – toe

(There's No Place Like)
HOME FOR THE HOLIDAYS

Words by AL STILLMAN
Music by ROBERT ALLEN

Oh, there's no place like Home For The

Hol - i - days; _____ 'Cause no mat - ter how

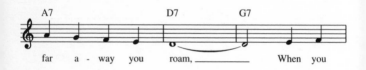

far a - way you roam, _____ When you

pine for the sun - shine of a

friend - ly gaze, _____ for the

hol - i - days you can't beat home sweet

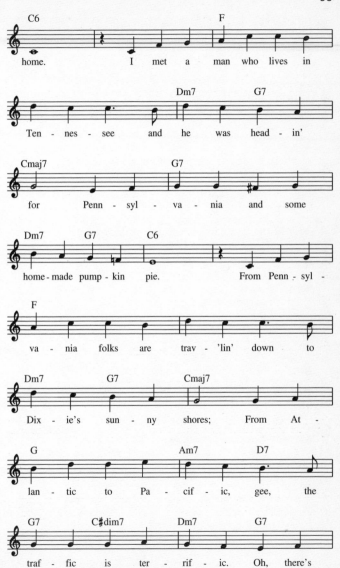

100

I HEARD THE BELLS ON CHRISTMAS DAY

Words by HENRY WADSWORTH LONGFELLOW
Adapted by JOHNNY MARKS
Music by JOHNNY MARKS

HOW LOVELY
IS CHRISTMAS

Words by ARNOLD SUNDGAARD
Music by ALEC WILDER

I SAW MOMMY KISSING SANTA CLAUS

Words and Music by
TOMMIE CONNOR

I STILL BELIEVE
IN SANTA CLAUS

Words and Music by MAURICE STARR
and AL LANCELLOTTI

I Still Be - lieve _ In San - ta Claus. _

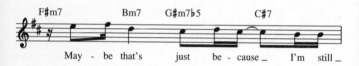

May - be that's just be - cause _ I'm still _

_ a child _ at heart. And I

still be - lieve _ in Old _ Saint Nick. _

Then a - gain, _ may - be that's _ the trick _

_ we need, _ we need to re - trieve _ from a

I WONDER AS I WANDER

By JOHN JACOB NILES

Espressivo

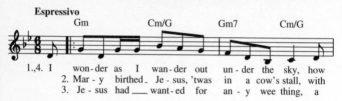

1.,4. I won-der as I wan-der out un-der the sky, how
2. Mar - y birthed Je - sus, 'twas in a cow's stall, with
3. Je - sus had want-ed for an - y wee thing, a

Je - sus the Sav - ior did come for to die for
wise men and farm - ers and shep-herds and all. But
star in the sky or a bird on the wing, or

poor on - 'ry peo - ple like you and like I... I
high from God's heav - en a star's light did fall, and the
all of God's an - gels in heav'n for to sing, He

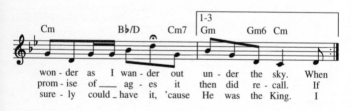

1-3

won - der as I wan - der out un - der the sky. When
prom - ise of ag - es it then did re - call. If
sure - ly could have it, 'cause He was the King. I

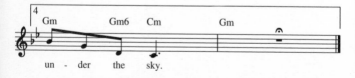

4

un - der the sky.

IT MUST HAVE
BEEN THE MISTLETOE
(Our First Christmas)

By JUSTIN WILDE
and DOUG KONECKY

It must have been __ the mis-tle-toe, __ the la-zy fire, __ the fall-ing snow, __ the mag-ic in __ the frost-y air, __ that feel - ing ev-'ry-where. It must have been __ the pret-ty lights __ that glis-tened __ in the si-lent night, __ or

110

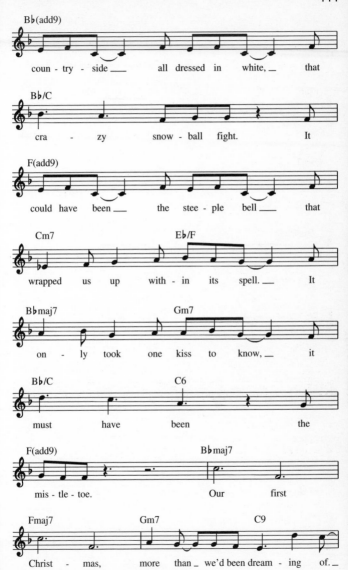

I'LL BE HOME
FOR CHRISTMAS

Words and Music by KIM GANNON
and WALTER KENT

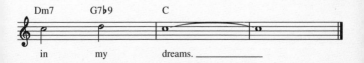

I'LL BE HOME
ON CHRISTMAS DAY

Words and Music by
MICHAEL JARRETT

Moderately slow

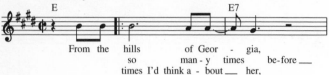

From the   hills   of Geor   -   gia,
so   man - y   times   be-fore ___
times I'd think a - bout ___ her,

a - cross   the   plains _____
she   left   that   can   -
all   the   love   I _____

___   of   Ten - nes   -   see, ___
- dle   burn - ing.
_____   left   be - hind.

I've   seen   and   I've   done _____
And   all   too _____
And   mem - o - ries _____

___   most   ev - 'ry - thing
___   man - y   tears   that   fell,
___   still   lin   -   ger

117

that a man can
my soul
with - in my

do or see.
filled with yearn - ing.
trou - bled mind.

But if I
If I had
If I could

could on - ly bor - row
an - y sense at all,
set a - side my pride,

one dream
I'd just be
then I'd be

from yes - ter - day,
on my way.
on my way.

I'd be on that train _____
I'd be on that train _____
I'd catch that train _____

_____ to - mor - row. }
_____ to - mor - row. }
_____ to - mor - row. }

I'll Be Home On _____

_____ Christ - mas Day. _____

1, 2

It's been
There were

3

If I had _____

_____ an - y sense at all, _____

I'd just be _____

I'M SPENDING CHRISTMAS WITH YOU

Words and Music by
TOM OCCHIPINTI

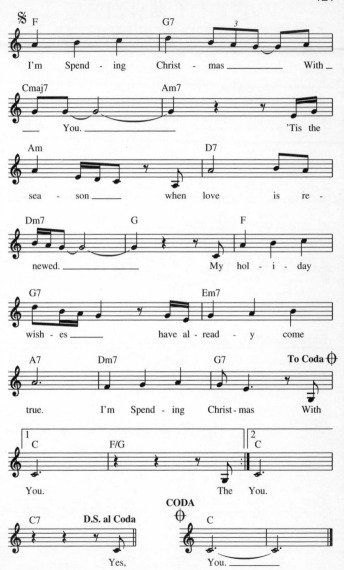

I'VE GOT MY LOVE TO KEEP ME WARM

from the 20th Century Fox Motion Picture ON THE AVENUE

Words and Music by
IRVING BERLIN

IT WON'T SEEM LIKE CHRISTMAS

(Without You)

Words and Music by
J.A. BALTHROP

Oh, it won't seem like Christ-mas, oh, with-out you, for too man-y miles are be-tween. But if I get the one thing that I'm wish-ing for then I'll see you to-night in my

125

dreams. Seems a long time ___ since

we've ___ been to-geth-er; ___ it was

just a - bout ___ to this time of year. ___

___ Looks like it's ___ gon-na

be ___ snow-y wea-ther. ___ How I

wish that you could be here. ___

But it dreams. In the

dis - tance   I   hear _____ sleigh bells

ring - ing.   The   hol - ly's _____ so

pret - ty _____ this   year   and   the

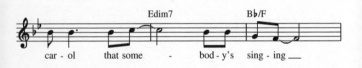

car - ol   that some   -   bod - y's   sing - ing ___

a - re - minds   me   of   our

Christ - mas   last   year.   Oh, ___ but   it

won't   be   like   Christ - mas   with -

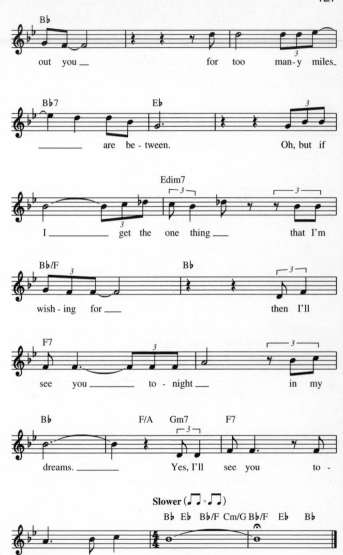

IT'S BEGINNING TO LOOK LIKE CHRISTMAS

By MEREDITH WILLSON

It's be-gin-ning to look a lot like Christ-mas,
ev - 'ry - where you go; { Take a / There's a
look in the five and ten, glis-ten-ing once a-gain, with
tree in the grand ho- tel, one in the park, as well, the
can - dy canes and sil - ver lanes a - glow. ___ } It's be-
stur - dy kind that does - n't mind the snow. ___
gin-ning to look a lot like Christ - mas,
{ toys in ev - 'ry store. But the
soon the bells will start. And the

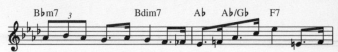

pret - ti - est sight to see is the hol - ly that will be on your
thing that will make them ring is the ca - rol that you sing right with-

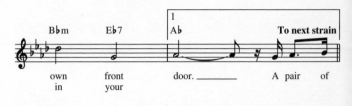

own   front   door. _____   A pair   of
in   your

heart. ____   hop-a-long boots and a pis-tol that shoots is the

wish   of Bar - ney   and   Ben;

Dolls that will talk and will go   for   a   walk   is   the

hope   of Jan - ice   and   Jen;   And

Mom and Dad can hard - ly wait for school to start a-gain. It's be -

IT'S CHRISTMAS TIME ALL OVER THE WORLD

Words and Music by
HUGH MARTIN

Fast and gaily

It's Christ - mas Time All

O - ver The World, _____ And

Christ - mas here at home. _____

_____ The church bells chime wher -

ev - er we roam, _____ So

Joy - eux No - ël,
(Zhwah - yuh No - el)

132

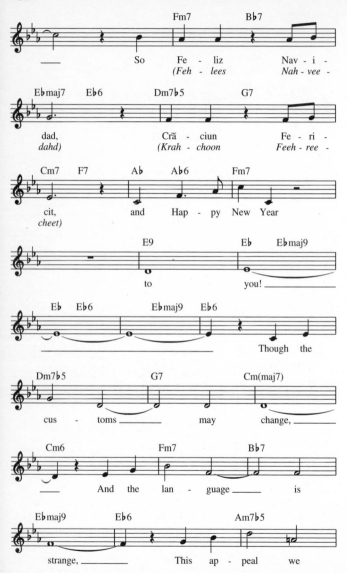

134

LAST CHRISTMAS

Words and Music by
GEORGE MICHAEL

136

JINGLE-BELL ROCK

Words and Music by JOE BEAL
and JIM BOOTHE

Moderately, with a rock beat

JINGLE, JINGLE, JINGLE

Music and Lyrics by
JOHNNY MARKS

THE LAST MONTH OF THE YEAR

(What Month Was Jesus Born In?)

Words and Music by VERA HALL
Adapted and Arranged by RUBY PICKENS TARTT
and ALAN LOMAX

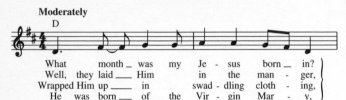

What month _ was my Je - sus born _ in?
Well, they laid _ Him in the man - ger,
Wrapped Him up _ in swad - dling cloth - ing,
He was born _ of the Vir - gin Mar - y,

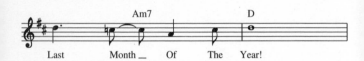

Last Month _ Of The Year!

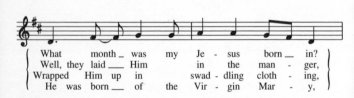

What month _ was my Je - sus born _ in?
Well, they laid Him in the man - ger,
Wrapped Him up in swad - dling cloth - ing,
He was born of the Vir - gin Mar - y,

Last Month _ Of The Year! _ Oh,

Jan - u - ar - y, Feb - ru - ar - y,

March, _____

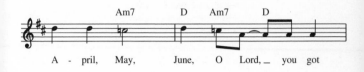

A - pril, May, June, O Lord, _ you got

Ju - ly, Aug - ust, Sep - tem - ber, Oc -

to - ber and - a No - vem - ber, On the

twen - ty - fifth day of De - cem - ber In The

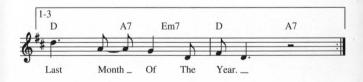

Last Month _ Of The Year. _

Last Month _ Of The Year. _____

LET IT SNOW!
LET IT SNOW!
LET IT SNOW!

Words by SAMMY CAHN
Music by JULE STYNE

Moderately

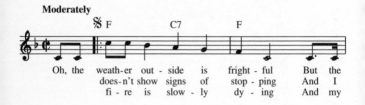

Oh, the weath-er out - side is fright - ful But the
does-n't show signs of stop - ping And I
fi - re is slow - ly dy - ing And my

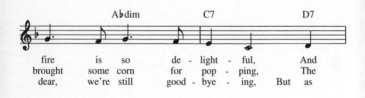

fire is so de - light - ful, And
brought some corn for pop - ping, The
dear, we're still good - bye - ing, But as

since we've no place to go,
lights are turned way down low, } Let It
long as you love me so,

C7

Snow! Let It Snow! Let It Snow! It

1
F

2
F   **To next strain**

3
F   **Fine**

Snow! When we Snow!

C   C#dim7

fi - nal-ly kiss good night How I'll

Dm7   G7   C

hate go - ing out in the storm! But if

Gm   A7

you'll real - ly hold me tight

D7   G7   C7   **D.S. al Fine**

All the way home I'll be warm. The

THE LITTLE BOY THAT SANTA CLAUS FORGOT

Words and Music by MICHAEL CARR,
TOMMY CONNOR and JIMMY LEACH

Slowly

Christ - mas comes but once a year for

ev - 'ry girl and boy, the

laugh - ter and the joy they

find in each new toy. I'll

tell you of a lit - tle boy who

lives a - cross the way; this

lit - tle fel - ler's Christ - mas is

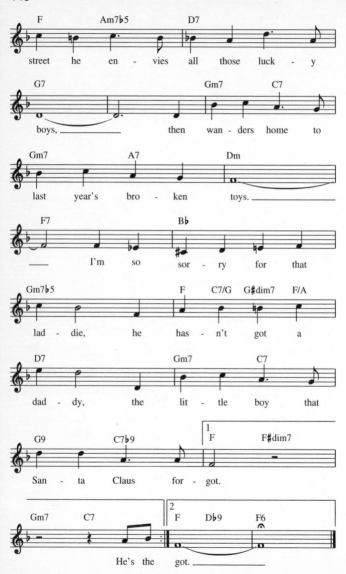

MERRY CHRISTMAS, DARLING

Words and Music by RICHARD CARPENTER
and FRANK POOLER

Rubato

Cm7 — Dm7 — Gm7

Greet - ing cards have all been sent,

Cm7 — F7 — Bb

the Christ - mas rush is through,

Gm — Gb+ — Bb/F — C/E

but I still have one wish to make,

Cm7 — F

a spe - cial one for you.

Moderately slow

Bbmaj9 — Cm/Bb

Mer - ry Christ - mas, dar - ling.

Bbmaj9 — Fm7 — Ab/Bb

We're a - part, that's true; but

150

151

LITTLE SAINT NICK

Words and Music by BRIAN WILSON
and MIKE LOVE

Moderately fast

Well,__ way up north where the air gets cold,__ there's a
lit-tle bob-sled, we call it Old Saint Nick,__ but she'll
haul-in' through the snow at a fright-'nin' speed__ with a

tale a-bout Christ-mas that you've all been told.__ And a
walk a to-bog-gan with a four speed stick.__ She's
half a doz-en deer__ with__ Ru-dy to lead. He's

real fa-mous cat all dressed up in red,__ and he
can-dy ap-ple red with a ski for a wheel, and when
got-ta wear his gog-gles 'cause the snow real-ly flies, and he's

spends the whole__ year work-in' out on his sled.__
San-ta hits the gas, man, just watch her__ peel.__ } It's the
cruis-in' ev-'ry pad with a lit-tle sur-prise.__

To Coda ⊕

Lit-tle Saint Nick. (Lit-tle Saint Nick.)__ It's the

1
D

Lit-tle Saint Nick. (Lit-tle Saint Nick.)__ Just a

A MARSHMALLOW WORLD

Words by CARL SIGMAN
Music by PETER DE ROSE

It's A Marsh-mal-low World in the win-ter _____ When the
snow comes to cov-er the ground. It's the
time for play, _ it's a whipped cream day, _ I
wait for it the whole year 'round. Those are
marsh-mal-low clouds be-ing friend-ly _____ in the
arms of the ev-er-green trees. And the
sun is red ___ like a pump-kin head; _ it's

MERRY CHRISTMAS, BABY

**Words and Music by LOU BAXTER
and JOHNNY MOORE**

got good mu-sic on my ra-di-o. _____ Well, I

want to kiss you, ba-by, while you're stand-in' 'neath the mis-tle-toe._

_____ Saint Nick came down the chim-ney 'bout

half - past three, _ left all these pret-ty pres-ents that you

see be-fore me. _ Mer-ry Christ-mas, lit-tle ba - by,

you sure _ been good to me. _____

_ I have-n't had a drink this morn-in', but I'm

all lit up like _ a Christ-mas tree. _____

MERRY CHRISTMAS FROM THE FAMILY

Words and Music by
ROBERT EARL KEEN

sang, "Fe - liz Na - vi - dad, _____ Fe - liz Na - vi -

dad." _____

Broth - er Ken brought his
Fran and Ri - ta drove from

kids with him, _ the three from his
Har - lin - gen. _ I can't re - mem-ber how I'm

first wife Lynn, and the two i -
kin to them. But when they tried to plug their

den - ti - cal twins _ from his sec - ond wife Mar - y
mo - tor-home in, _ they _ blew our _ Christ - mas

Nell. _____ 'Course he brought his
lights. _____ Cous - in Da - vid knew just

ten - sion   chord, ___   a can of bean dip and some
can of   fake snow,   a bag of lem-ons and some

Di - et   Rites, ___   a box of tam - pons ___ and some
Di - et   Sprites, ___   a box of tam - pons ___ and some

Marl - bo - ro Lights. }
Sa - lem ___ Lights. }   Hal - le - lu - jah, ev - 'ry -

bod - y say "cheese."   Mer - ry Christ - mas ___ from the

fam - i - ly. ___

fam - i -

ly. ___

Fe - liz   Na - vi - dad.

THE MERRY CHRISTMAS POLKA

Words by PAUL FRANCIS WEBSTER
Music by SONNY BURKE

Come on and dance The Mer-ry Christ-mas
dance The Mer-ry Christ-mas

Pol-ka, Let ev-'ry-one be
Pol-ka, Let ev-'ry la-dy

hap-py and gay, _____ Oh! it's the
step with her beau _____ A-round a

time to be jol-ly and
tree to the ceil-ing with

deck the halls with hol-ly, So
lots of time for steal-ing, Those

let's have a jol-ly hol-i-
kiss-es be-neath the mis-tle-

163

MERRY MERRY CHRISTMAS, BABY

Words and Music by MARGO SYLVIA
and GIL LOPEZ

Slow '50s Rock

Mer - ry mer - ry Christ-mas, ba - by. _____

Al-though you're with some - bod-y new, _____

thought I'd send a card to say that I wish this _ hol - i -

day would find me _____ be - side _ you. _____

Mer - ry mer - ry Christ-mas, ba - by, _____
Instrumental

and a hap - py _ New Year too. _____

It was Christ-mas Eve we met, a hol-i-day I __ can't for-

get, 'cause that's when we fell in love. _____
Instrumental ends

I still ____ re-mem-ber _____

the gifts we gave ___ to each oth-er. _____

This love I hold _____ with-in my

heart _____ still grows, though we're ___ a-

part. Have a Mer-ry Christ-mas, ba-by, _____

and a Hap-py _ New Year too. _____

I am hop-ing that you'll find a _ love as _ true as

mine. Mer-ry mer-ry Christ-mas, ba - by. _____

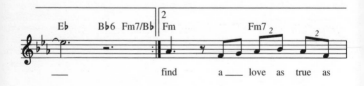

_ find a _ love as true as

mine. Mer-ry mer-ry Christ-mas, ba - by. _____

_

MISS YOU MOST
AT CHRISTMAS TIME

Words and Music by MARIAH CAREY
and WALTER AFANASIEFF

With feeling

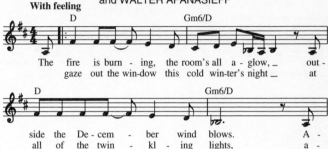

The fire is burn - ing, the room's all a - glow, _ out -
gaze out the win - dow this cold win-ter's night _ at

side the De - cem - ber wind blows. A -
all of the twin - kl - ing lights, a -

way in the dis - tance the car - ol - ers sing _ in the snow.
lone in the dark - ness, re - mem-ber-ing when _ you were mine.

Ev - 'ry-bod-y's laugh-ing, the world is cel - e - brat-ing and
Ev - 'ry-bod-y's smil-ing, the whole world is re - joic-ing and

ev - 'ry-one's so hap - py _ ex - cept for me to-night, be-cause ⎱ I
ev - 'ry-one's em-brac-ing _ ex - cept for you and I. Ba - by, ⎰

miss you most at _ Christ-mas time _ and I can't _

MISTER SANTA

Words and Music by
PAT BALLARD

1. Mis - ter San - ta, bring { me / us } some toys
2.,3. *(See additional lyrics)*

bring Mer - ry Christ - mas to

all girls and boys. And ev - 'ry

night { I'll / we'll } go to sleep sing - ing

and dream a - bout the pres - ents you'll be

bring - ing. San - ta, prom - ise { me / us } please,

give ev - 'ry rein - deer a

hug and a squeeze. {I'll / We'll} be good, __ as good can

be, _____ Mis - ter San - ta don't for - get me. __

Mis - ter

Additional Lyrics

2. Mister Santa, dear old Saint Nick
   Be awful careful and please don't get sick
   Put on your coat when breezes are blowin'
   And when you cross the street look where you're goin'.
   Santa, we (I) love you so,
   We (I) hope you never get lost in the snow.
   Take your time when you unpack,
   Mister Santa don't hurry back.

3. Mister Santa, we've been so good
   We've washed the dishes and done what we should.
   Made up the beds and scrubbed up our toesies,
   We've used a kleenex when we've blown our nosesies.
   Santa look at our ears, they're clean as whistles,
   We're sharper than shears
   Now we've put you on the spot,
   Mister Santa bring us a lot.

THE NIGHT BEFORE CHRISTMAS SONG

Music by JOHNNY MARKS
Lyrics adapted by JOHNNY MARKS
from Clement Moore's Poem

174

NUTTIN' FOR CHRISTMAS

Words and Music by ROY BENNETT
and SID TEPPER

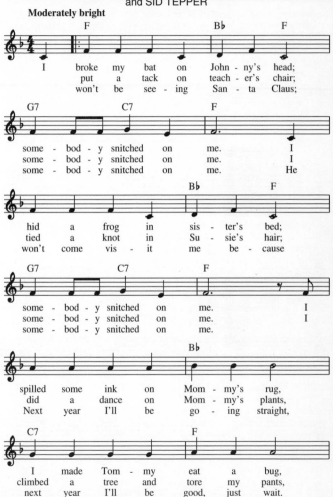

I broke my bat on Johnny's head;
put a tack on teacher's chair;
won't be seeing Santa Claus;

some-bod-y snitched on me. I
some-bod-y snitched on me. I
some-bod-y snitched on me. He

hid a frog in sister's bed;
tied a knot in Susie's hair;
won't come visit me because

some-bod-y snitched on me. I
some-bod-y snitched on me. I
some-bod-y snitched on me.

spilled some ink on Mommy's rug,
did a dance on Mommy's plants,
Next year I'll be going straight,

I made Tommy eat a bug,
climbed a tree and tore my pants,
next year I'll be good, just wait.

Dm   G7

Bought   some   gum   with   a   pen - ny   slug;
Filled   the   sug - ar ____   bowl   with   ants;
I'd   start   now   but ____   it's   too   late;

C7   F   C7

some - bod - y   snitched   on   me.   Oh.   }
some - bod - y   snitched   on   me.   So,   }
some - bod - y   snitched   on   me.   Oh,   }

F

I'm   get - tin'   Nut - tin'   For

                            C7

Christ - mas.   Mom - my   and

Dad - dy   are   mad.

F

I'm   get - tin'   Nut - tin'   For

Christ - mas,   'Cause

177

AN OLD FASHIONED CHRISTMAS

Music and Lyrics by
JOHNNY MARKS

ONE BRIGHT STAR

Words and Music by
JOHN JARVIS

181

PLEASE COME HOME FOR CHRISTMAS

Words and Music by CHARLES BROWN and GENE REDD

185

PRETTY PAPER

Words and Music by
WILLIE NELSON

187

ROCKIN' AROUND THE CHRISTMAS TREE

Music and Lyrics by
JOHNNY MARKS

Moderate Rock

Rock-in' A-round The Christ-mas Tree _ at the
Christ-mas par-ty hop, _ Mis-tle-toe hung where
you can see _ ev-'ry cou-ple tries to stop.
Rock-in' A-round The Christ-mas Tree, _ let the
Christ-mas spir-it ring. _ Lat-er we'll have some
pun-kin pie _ and we'll do some car-ol-
ing. You will get a sen-ti-men-tal

RUDOLPH THE RED-NOSED REINDEER

Music and Lyrics by
JOHNNY MARKS

Verse (ad lib.)

You know Dash - er and Danc - er and

Pranc - er and Vix - en, Com - et and Cu - pid and

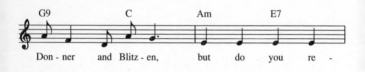

Don - ner and Blitz - en, but do you re -

call the most fa - mous rein - deer of

Chorus (a tempo)

all?   Ru - dolph The Red - nosed
       All of the oth - er

191

Rein - deer had a ver - y shin - y
rein - deer used to laugh and call him

nose, and if you ev - er
names, they nev - er let poor

saw it, you would e - ven say it
Ru - dolph

glows. join in an - y rein - deer

games. Then one fog - gy

Christ - mas Eve, San - ta came to

say, "Ru - dolph, with your

nose so bright, won't you guide my

sleigh to - night?"_ Then how the rein - deer

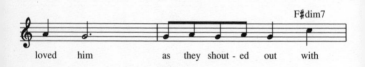

loved him as they shout - ed out with

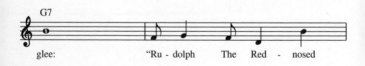

glee: "Ru - dolph The Red - nosed

Rein - deer, you'll go down in

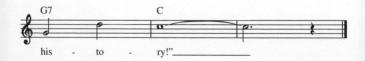

his - to - ry!"_____

SANTA BABY

By JOAN JAVITS, PHIL SPRINGER
and TONY SPRINGER

Moderately slow

Mis - ter "Claus," I feel as tho' I know ya. _____ So

you won't mind if I should get fam - il - ya, will ya?

San - ta Ba - by, just slip a sa - ble un - der the tree __
San - ta Ba - by, one lit - tle thing I real - ly do need; __

__ for me. __ Been an aw - ful good girl, __
__ The deed __ to a plat - i - num mine,

__ San - ta Ba - by, So hur - ry down the chim - ney to - night. __
__ San - ta hon - ey, So hur - ry down the chim - ney to - night,

San - ta Ba - by, a
San - ta cu - tie, and

fif - ty - four con - vert - i - ble, too, ___
fill my stock - ing with a du - plex ___

___ light blue. ___ I'll wait up for you, dear ___
___ and cheques. ___ Sign your X on the line, ___

___ San - ta Ba - by, so hur - ry down the chim - ney to - night. ___
___ San - ta cu - tie, and hur - ry down the chim - ney to - night. ___

Think of all the
Come and trim my

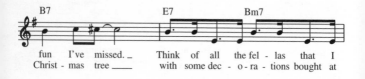

fun I've missed. ___ Think of all the fel - las that I
Christ - mas tree ___ with some dec - o - ra - tions bought at

have - n't kissed. ___ Next year I could be
Tif - fa - ny. ___ I real - ly do be -

SANTA, BRING MY BABY BACK (TO ME)

Words and Music by CLAUDE DeMETRUIS and AARON SCHROEDER

Don't need a lot of pres - ents to make my Christ - mas bright. But
Christ - mas tree is read - y, the can - dles all a - glow. You
fill my sock with can - dy, no bright and shin - y toy.

I just need my ba - by's arms wound a - round me tight. Oh,
with my ba - by far a - way what good is mis - tle - toe? Then
wan - na make me hap - py and fill my heart with joy. } San - ta,

hear my plea. _____

San - ta, Bring My Ba - by Back To

SHAKE ME I RATTLE

(Squeeze Me I Cry)

Words and Music by HAL HACKADY
and CHARLES NAYLOR

Moderately slow

I was pass - ing by a toy shop on the
called an - oth - er toy shop on a
late and snow was fall - ing as the

cor - ner of the Square, where a
square so long a - go, where I
shop - pers hur - ried by past the

lit - tle girl was look - ing in the win - dow
saw a lit - tle dol - ly that I want - ed
girl - ie at the win - dow with her lit - tle head held

there. She was look - ing at a
so. I re - mem - bered, I re -
high. They were clos - ing up the

dol - ly in a dress of ros - y
mem - bered how I longed to make it
toy shop as I hur - ried thru the

red, and a - round the pret - ty
mine, and a - round that oth - er
door, just in time to buy the

SHARE LOVE

Words and Music by
NATHAN MORRIS

It's that time of the year a - gain ___ for ___ you
Fam - 'lies all ___ a - round, ___ chil - dren are
___ to share ___ all the
hap - py with what they found,
love ___ that you have ___ with ev - 'ry wom -
giv - ing things on this day ___ and thank - ing our God,
- an and ev - 'ry man, ___ to share ___ love.
___ for teach - ing us the way to share ___ love.
___
As the
Christ - mas Day ___ is here ___ and the Lord ___
snow is fall - ing down, pres - ents un - wrapped un -

SILVER AND GOLD

Music and Lyrics by
JOHNNY MARKS

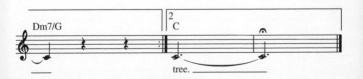

SILVER BELLS

from the Paramount Picture THE LEMON DROP KID

*Words and Music by JAY LIVINGSTON
and RAY EVANS*

SOME CHILDREN SEE HIM

Lyric by WIHLA HUTSON
Music by ALFRED BURT

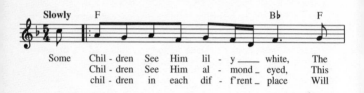

Some Chil - dren See Him lil - y ____ white, The
Chil - dren See Him al - mond _ eyed, This
chil - dren in each dif - f'rent _ place Will

Ba - by Je - sus ____ born this night. Some
Sav - iour whom we ____ kneel be - side. Some
see the Ba - by ____ Je - sus' face Like

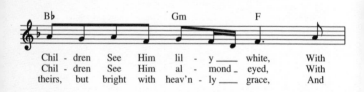

Chil - dren See Him lil - y ____ white, With
Chil - dren See Him al - mond _ eyed, With
theirs, but bright with heav'n - ly ____ grace, And

tress - es soft and ____ fair. Some
skin of yel - low ____ hue. Some
filled with ho - ly ____ light. O

C   Dm7   Am

Chil - dren   See   Him __ bronzed and brown,   The
Chil - dren   See   Him __ dark   as   they,   Sweet
lay   a - side   each   earth - ly   thing,   And

Bb   Ab   Bb/C

Lord   of   heav'n   to __ earth   came   down;   Some
Mar - y's   Son   to __ whom   we   pray;   Some
with   thy   heart   as __ of - fer - ing,   Come

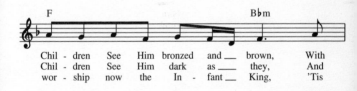

F   Bbm

Chil - dren   See   Him bronzed and __ brown,   With
Chil - dren   See   Him dark   as __ they,   And
wor - ship   now   the   In - fant __ King,   'Tis

1,2
Bb   Gm7   F

dark   and   heav - y __ hair.   Some
ah!   they   love   him __ too!   The

3
Bb   Gm7   F

love   that's   born   to - night!

THE STAR CAROL

Lyric by WIHLA HUTSON
Music by ALFRED BURT

Tenderly, with much expression

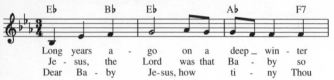

Long years a - go on a deep _ win - ter
Je - sus, the Lord was that Ba - by so
Dear Ba - by Je - sus, how ti - ny Thou

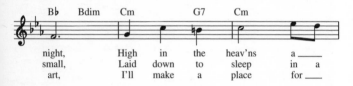

night, High in the heav'ns a _____
small, Laid down to sleep in a
art, I'll make a place for _____

star _____ shone bright, While in a
hum - ble stall; Then came the
Thee _ in my heart, And when the

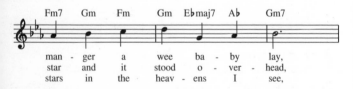

man - ger a wee ba - by lay,
star and it stood o - ver - head,
stars in the heav - ens I see,

Sweet - ly a - sleep on a bed of hay.
Shed - ding its light 'round His lit - tle bed.
Ev - er and al - ways I'll think of Thee.

WHAT A MERRY CHRISTMAS THIS COULD BE

Words and Music by HANK COCHRAN and HARLAN HOWARD

What a Mer - ry Christ - mas this could be if you ___ would just come back ___ to ___ me ___ and say that you'd for - giv - en. ___ me. ___ What a Mer - ry Christ - mas this ___ could ___ be. ___ It was just ___ last Christ - mas that we

212

quar-reled and you walked out. ___ I knew

I was wrong, ___ but you'd ___ come

back; I ___ had no doubt. Now a year

___ has rolled a - round, ___ it's

Christ-mas once a - gain, and

what I'd give if you'd ___ come ___ walk - in' ___

___ in. What a Mer -

(1.,3.) - ry Christ - mas this could
(2.) *Instrumental*

be   if   you ___   would

just come back __ to __ me ___   and

say   that   you'd   for - giv - en __

__ me. _____   What   a   Mer -

- ry   Christ - mas   this ___   could _

1,2

__ be. _____   *Instrumental*

Instrumental ends What   a   Mer -

3

What   a   Mer - ry

Christ - mas   this _   could _ be. _____

SUZY SNOWFLAKE

Words and Music by SID TEPPER
and ROY BENNETT

Moderately

Here comes Su - zy Snow - flake,
Here comes Su - zy Snow - flake,

dressed in a snow white gown,
soon you will hear her say,

Tap, tap, tap - pin' at your win - dow pane to
"Come out, ev - 'ry - one, and play with me; I

tell you she's in town.

have – n't long to stay.

If you wan - na make a snow man,

I'll help you make one one, two three.

THIS ONE'S FOR THE CHILDREN

Words and Music by
MAURICE STARR

Slowly

There are some peo - ple _____
Man - y peo - ple are hap - py _____ and

liv - ing in ____ this world; _____
man - y peo - ple are sad. _____

they have no food to eat, _____ they
Some peo - ple have man - y things _ that

have no place _____ to go. ____
oth - ers can on - ly ____ wish ____ they had.

But we all are God's chil - dren, we have to
So, for the sake of the chil - dren, show _

learn to love _ one an - oth - er. _____
_ them love's the on - ly way to go _____

Gm7
F/A
Just re - mem - ber they could be us Re -
'cause they're our to - mor - row, and
Bbmaj7
C
mem - ber we all are broth - ers.
peo - ple they've got to know.
Bbmaj7
3
Bbmaj7/C
I'm not try - ing to
Fmaj7
dark - en up your day,
Ebmaj9#11
3
but help oth - ers in need and
Gm7
C7sus
show them there's a bet - ter way.
Bb/C
Bb
Am7
Dm7
This One's For The Chil - dren,

WE NEED A LITTLE CHRISTMAS

from MAME

Music and Lyric by
JERRY HERMAN

Brightly

Haul out the hol - ly, _____
climb down the chim - ney, _____

_____ put up the tree be - fore my
_____ turn on the bright - est string of

spir - it falls _____ a - gain; Fill
lights I've ev - er seen; Slice

up the stock - ing, _____ I may be
up the fruit - cake, _____ it's time we

rush - ing things, but deck the halls _____
hung some tin - sel on the ev -

_____ a - gain now. _____
- er - green bough. _____

WHAT ARE YOU DOING NEW YEAR'S EVE?

By FRANK LOESSER

Slowly and sentimentally

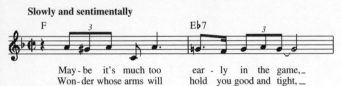

May - be it's much too ear - ly in the game, _
Won - der whose arms will hold you good and tight, _

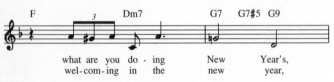

ah, but I thought I'd ask you just the same, _
when it's ex - act - ly twelve o' - clock that night, _

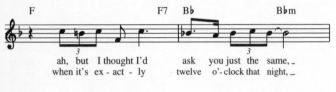

what are you do - ing New Year's,
wel - com - ing in the new year,

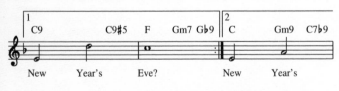

New Year's Eve? New Year's

Eve. May - be I'm cra - zy

to sup - pose I'd ev - er be the

one   you   chose.   Out of the thou - sand

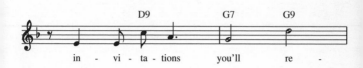

in - vi - ta - tions   you'll   re -

ceive.   Ah, but in case I

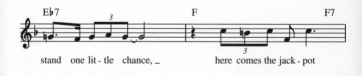

stand one lit - tle chance, __   here comes the jack - pot

ques - tion in ad - vance, __   what are you do - ing

New   Year's,   New   Year's   Eve?

WHAT CHRISTMAS MEANS TO ME

Words and Music by GEORGE GORDY, ALLEN STORY and ANNA GORDY GAYE

Brightly

Can - dles burn - in' low,

lots of mis - tle - toe,

lots of snow ___ and ice,

ev - 'ry - where ___ we go.

Choirs ___ sing - in' car - ols

right out - side ___ my door.

Dm7

All these things and more,

(All these things and more, _____ ba - by.) that's what Christ -

F/G

- mas means _ to me, _____ my love. (That's what

Christ - mas means to me, _____ my love.) _

N.C.

(Instrumental)

C

I _____ see your smil - ing face

F   C

like I nev - er seen _ be - fore._

____ my love. (That's what Christ - mas means to me, ____

____ my love.)____ I feel ____ like run -

- nin' wild, ____ as anx - ious as a

lit - tle child to greet ____ you 'neath ____ the mis -

- tle - toe, kiss you once ____ and then ____

____ some more. And wish you a mer - ry Christ -

- mas, ba - by,

(Wish you a mer - ry Christ -

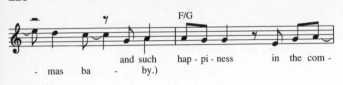

and such hap-pi-ness in the com-
-mas ba - by.)

-ing year. ___ Whoa, ba -

- by. Let's deck ___ the halls ___ with hol -

- ly, sing sweet "Si - lent Night."

Fill a tree ___ with an -

- gel hair ___ and pret-ty, pret - ty lights. ___

___ Go to sleep ___ and wake ___

_ up just be - fore _ day - light. _

_ And all _ these things and more, _

_ ba - by, (All these things and more, _

that's _ what Christ - mas means _ to me, _
_ ba - by.)

_ my love. (That's what Christ - mas means to me, _

_ my love.) _ (Instrumental)

Repeat ad lib. and Fade

WHEN LOVE CAME DOWN

Written by CHRIS EATON

Moderately fast

Christ - mas Eve, _____ two a. m.; _____
we can breathe; _____

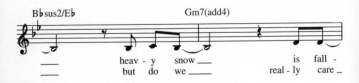

_____ heav - y snow _____ is fall -
_____ but do we _____ real - ly care

- ing down. And the streets _____ clothed in
for this world _____ in _____ need? _____ There's a

white _____ ech - o songs, _____ that were sung
choice _____ we must make _____ each and ev -

_____ by can - dle - light. _____

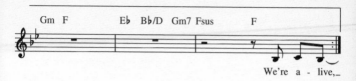

We're a - live,_

- 'ry day. _ So, close your eyes _ and share_

_ the _ dream; _ let ev - 'ry - one _ on earth _

_ be - lieve. _ The Child was born, _ the stars _

_ shone _ bright, _ and Love came down _ at Christ-

- mas time, _ and Love came down _ at Christ-

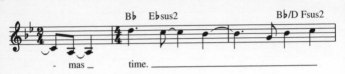

Bb **Eb sus2** **Bb/D Fsus2**

- mas __ time. _____

Gm7 **Eb sus2** **Gm** **F**

Oh, ___ yeah, ___ yeah. ___

Bb **Eb sus2** **Bb/D** **Fsus2**

Time. _____

Gm7 **Eb sus2** **Gm** **F**

Oh, ___ yeah, ___ yeah. _   So,

F **Bb** **Eb sus2**

Mer - ry Christ - mas ev - 'ry - one, __   and

F **Bb**

peace through - out __ the   year. _____   The

233

time has come to cel - e - brate, So

let your voic - es fill the air.

Ev - 'ry - one, watch and pray

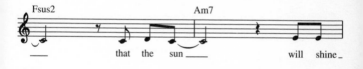

that the sun will shine

on a bright - er day. Join your hands,

lift them high for this gift

of life. When Love came down at

234

THE WHITE WORLD OF WINTER

Words by MITCHELL PARISH
Music by HOAGY CARMICHAEL

Moderately with a lift

In this won - der - ful white world of
won - der - ful white world of

win - ter _____ Dar - ling,
win - ter _____ Dar - ling,

we'll have a won - der - ful
we'll have a won - der - ful

time; _____ First, we'll
time; _____ If we

ride side by side thru the
prayed it would snow all this

hin - ter _____ And ron - de -
win - ter _____ I ask ya,

236

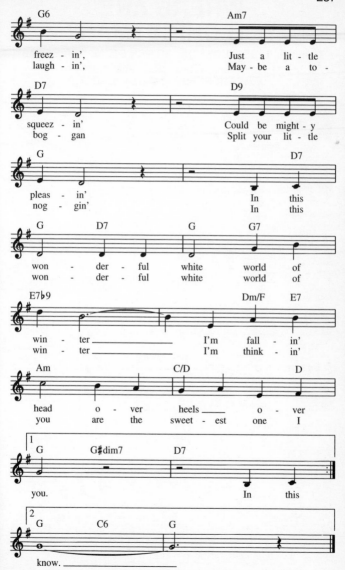

WHERE ARE YOU CHRISTMAS?

from DR. SEUSS' HOW THE GRINCH STOLE CHRISTMAS

Words and Music by WILL JENNINGS,
JAMES HORNER and MARIAH CAREY

WHO WOULD IMAGINE A KING

from the Touchstone Motion Picture THE PREACHER'S WIFE

Words and Music by MERVYN WARREN
and HALLERIN HILTON HILL

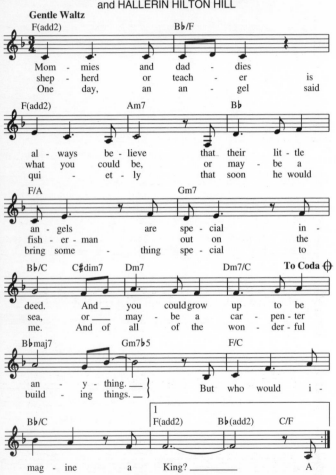

Gentle Waltz

Mom - mies and dad - dies al - ways be - lieve that their lit - tle
an - gels are spe - cial in - deed. And __ you could grow up to be
an - y - thing. __ But who would i - mag - ine a King? __

shep - herd or teach - er is what you could be, or may - be a
fish - er - man out on the sea, or __ may - be a car - pen - ter
build - ing things. __

One day, an an - gel said qui - et - ly that soon he would
bring some - thing spe - cial to me. And of all of the won - der - ful

244

WHY CHRISTMAS

Words and Music by
WANYA MORRIS

Slow R&B

Ev - 'ry day __ at this time of __ year I
No one was there but Grand - ma __ and her __ friends; a

won - der time __ and time __ a - gain, __ why are kids __
time of heart - ache is set - ting in. __ There's

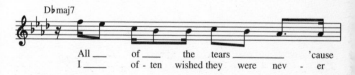

__ suf - fer-ing? __
__ noth - in' I can __ do, just sit __ and feel __ pain run __ me through. __

All __ of __ the tears _____ 'cause
I __ of - ten wished they were nev - er

be - ing caught __ in the __ cross - fi - re. _____
born. The thought of them not having no toys. Their little hearts were torn.

__ Some - bod -
I was young and I cried __

- y tell __ me __ why. As _____
__ as well. _____

Dbmaj7

___ the joy - ous day __ comes a - long, the
I did - n't have a job, __ but I prayed to the

eld - est feel __ there's some - thing wrong. _ He's
Lord that there'd be bet - ter days. Yes, he gave me a

Fm7

look - in' for mom __ but she's __ not there. _ Kids are
rea - son to live, he gave me a sign. _____ But I

Eb/G

look - ing for rein - deer in __ the air. _____
still think to __ that day __ when _____ }

Absus(add2)

She messed up a - gain. _____

%

Abmaj9   **Dbmaj7**

Why? _ My _ broth - er and _ my sis - ter,

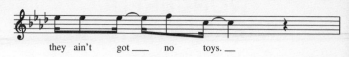

they ain't got ___ no toys. ___

What am I ___ sup - posed ___ to do ___ when grow-ing

up for me ___ was-n't joy? ___ It's gon - na be a

why ___ Christ - mas. ___ It's gon -

- na be, ___ it's gon - na be ___ a, a

why ___ Christ - mas. ___

My ___

WONDERFUL CHRISTMASTIME

Words and Music by
McCARTNEY

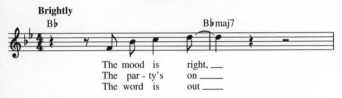

The mood is right, ___
The par-ty's on ___
The word is out ___

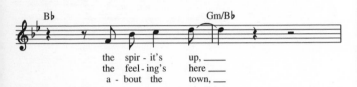

the spir-it's up, ___
the feel-ing's here ___
a-bout the town, ___

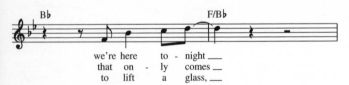

we're here to-night ___
that on-ly comes ___
to lift a glass, ___

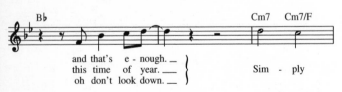

and that's e-nough. ___
this time of year. ___
oh don't look down. ___

Sim-ply

hav-ing a won-der-ful Christ-mas-

time. Sim - ply hav - ing a
won - der - ful Christ - mas - time. time.

The choir of chil - dren
sing their song. *(2nd time only)* (They prac - tised

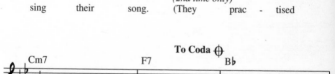

To Coda ⊕

all year long.) Ding

dong, ding dong. Ding dong, ding.

Ooh _____ Ooh _____

Do do   do   do   do do   do

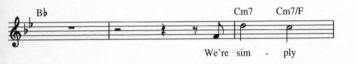

We're sim - ply

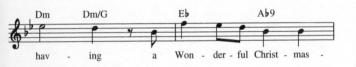

hav - ing   a   Won - der - ful Christ - mas -

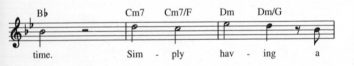

time.   Sim - ply   hav - ing   a

D.C. al Coda   **CODA**

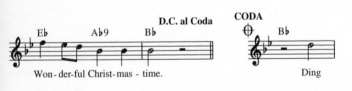

Won - der - ful Christ - mas - time.   Ding

dong,   ding   dong,   ding   dong,   ding

GUITAR CHORD FRAMES

This guitar chord reference includes 120 commonly used chords. For a more complete guide to guitar chords, see "THE PAPERBACK CHORD BOOK" (HL00702009).

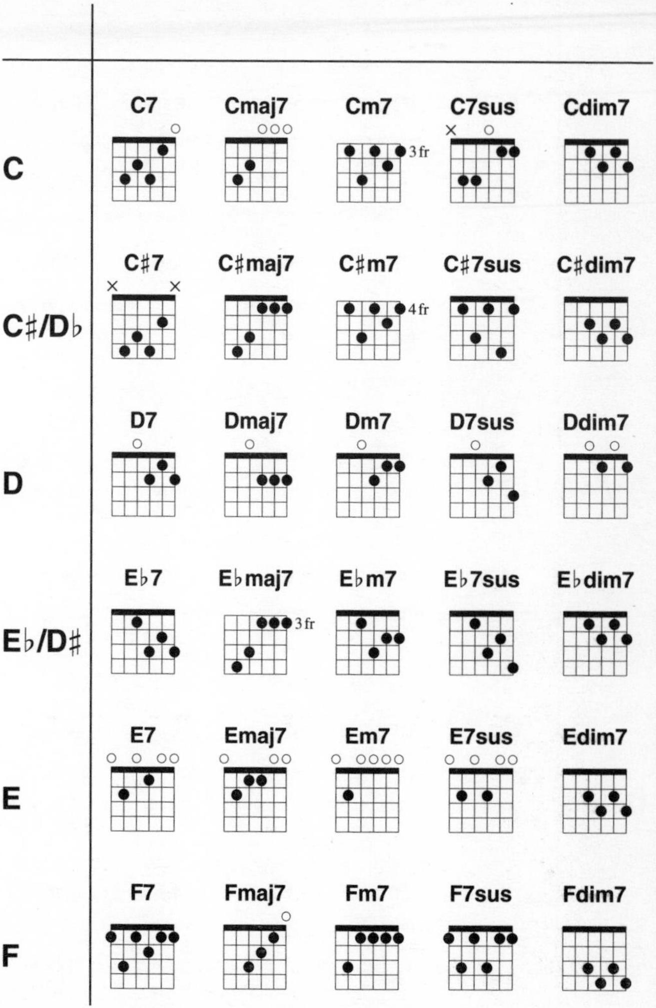
C
C7
Cmaj7
Cm7
3 fr
C7sus
Cdim7
C♯/D♭
C♯7
C♯maj7
C♯m7
4 fr
C♯7sus
C♯dim7
D
D7
Dmaj7
Dm7
D7sus
Ddim7
E♭/D♯
E♭7
E♭maj7
3 fr
E♭m7
E♭7sus
E♭dim7
E
E7
Emaj7
Em7
E7sus
Edim7
F
F7
Fmaj7
Fm7
F7sus
Fdim7

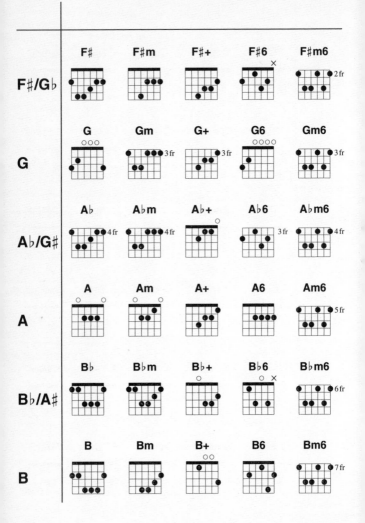